MY JOB OFFER NEGOTIATION SKILLS ARE SOLID

I think

...SO WHY DIDN'T I GET ANYTHING I ASKED FOR?

I0463219

Easy guide for people with 5+ years of professional work experience to evaluate and negotiate the details of a *job offer*

STACIE GARLIEB

Copyright © 2010 Stacie Garlieb

ISBN: 1450510205

ISBN-13: 9781450510202

TABLE OF CONTENTS

I think

INTRODUCTION

You successfully answered the questions in a phone interview, a live interview (or several) and the company just called to make you a job offer! Receiving an offer for a job opportunity is exciting – so how can you determine if it's a 'good' offer? What are the important parts of an offer to understand? How can you negotiate parts of an offer? When and how do you notify other companies when you accept an offer?

The 'we' in the book is referring to a combined collaboration of recruiters, HR managers, and hiring managers who are currently in positions interviewing candidates daily. 'We' make offers to candidates every month, and have heard almost every question about an offer asked in appropriate and inappropriate ways.

Understanding what a company is truly offering you, beyond a paycheck, is important for you to evaluate which job opportunity fits your goals and career objectives at the time. As you go through each section of the book, figure out what areas you will use at this point in your career. This book can be a reference for tips as you receive and negotiate promotions, lateral positions between departments, or relocation.

My comprehension of what to do when

I 'get the call' is good **I think** ...

In **'My interview skills are strong I think ...so why didn't I get the job offer?'** © we noted one key to successfully working through the phone interview process is to make sure you are in the 'right place at the right time' for the interview. And similar to that scenario, taking a call from an employer about a job offer when you are driving down the freeway, or sitting in a loud office is not a good strategy.

The best way to be prepared when you 'get the call' is to not answer your phone if you don't recognize the number. Recruiters and hiring managers will leave you a message. We know you have other things going on and it's not a problem if we talk to you right then, or in an hour when you are in a better place to have a professional conversation.

Before you call the person back, make sure you have these things in front of you:

- Pad of paper to take some quick notes
  - Look at the list in the next section of the book for some basic categories of information you may be told via phone about an offer

- Job description that you applied and interviewed for
  - This lets you verify the title of the job and some basic information

- ◆ Any specific notes you took at career fairs, during the interviews, or found online through the company's website about the compensation package

The first thing the hiring person will tell you is 'We would like to make you an offer'. They may pause to see your reaction – this is a good time to say 'Thank you, I am very excited to hear from you'. Then most likely you be given some very topline information about the position – title, base salary, what overall is included in a 'benefits' package, and what else you have to do to officially secure the job.

It is very normal for companies to ask for the following as 'contingent on completion for employment':

- ◆ Background check
- ◆ Drug test
- ◆ Driver's License check (depends on the job)
- ◆ Completion of an I-9 Form – verification of ability to work in the US

Once the person finishes telling you the basics of the offer, it's important to respond and give them a signal of how you are interpreting the offer at this point. Unless you have already decided **not** to accept the offer, you can respond with a simple statement like "I appreciate the offer. Could you please send me the details via email or fax so I can see what questions I may have?". This allows you to see the offer in writing and then determine what you want to do – ask questions, negotiate parts, accept, or reject it.

Usually the hiring person will give you a deadline of when they need to hear back from you. By setting a deadline, we can hire our next choice if you reject the offer. Timelines also set a sense of urgency to you as the candidate, as a way to get you to commit faster.

• • •

My awareness of what to look for in an offer is complete I think ...

All job offers have some basic parts, but each offer will also have different 'extras' or 'benefits' based on the level of responsibility for the position, size of the company, and current market trends for the industry or job title. The most common parts of a job offer include:

- Salary – hourly, base (annual or weekly or bi-weekly), contract pay – paid at the end of a given time period
- Medical benefits
    - Medical could include general medical, dental, vision care or a combination of any of those

- Vacation/Sick day benefits
- Insurance benefits – short and/or long term care, life insurance
- 'Bonus' compensation
    - Usually based on achieving goals and could be tied to several different criteria

- 401K and/or retirement/pension plan
- 'Signing bonus'
- Mileage reimbursement or Car Allowance or Company car
- Business Expense reimbursement
- Relocation allowance or reimbursement
- Start Date

* Location of the position (geographic or department)
* Timing for performance evaluation and review of merit increase to base salary (quarterly, annual)

Not every job offer will have all of these parts. Doing some homework before the offer is presented to you will help to know what is reasonable for the position. For example, a salesperson would probably have some form of 'bonus' to increase motivation to sell more, while someone in an operations position in a manufacturing plant may not. Some of these benefits may be offered in higher levels of an organization's career paths. Several Fortune 500 companies that used to give salespeople a company car in the past are now giving mileage reimbursement or a car allowance until the person reaches a management level.

Here are a few of these items in greater detail so you can see some general guidelines and differences:

* **Salary**
  As you move higher in an organization or take on additional responsibility, it is important to understand how the salary range for the position relates to trends in the industry or geography.

* **Medical benefits**
  Two very important things to look for here:

  1) When do the benefits start?
     It's not unusual for a company to start benefits after 90 days of employment ('the probationary period'), so plan on what you can do to bridge your coverage during this time. If you have been working at another company, you could potentially contact that medical carrier and see what arrangements you could make for the three months.

2) What exactly is covered?
   Dental benefits may not be included, vision may not be included, etc. so again be sure if you need a certain level of coverage that you are looking for that in the offer.

It may also be important for you to retain your current medical provider for you or your dependents. If this is the case, once you receive the offer in writing be sure to contact your provider to determine if they accept the health plan(s) being offered to you by the company.

- **Vacation/Sick Day benefits**
  Some companies will give vacation time after a certain amount of 'time in the job'. This could also be considered 'accrued vacation'. So, if you start the position in June, possibly you would 'accrue' one day of vacation after each month of employment – which means that on December 1st you would have six days of 'accrued vacation'.

  Other companies will give a flat number of vacation days each year, based on number of years you have worked there. Two weeks is typical for a company to offer to a new employee. The company can set a time period and different times during the year that vacation is or is not approved. There also may be 'forced' vacation times, for example some organizations 'close down' between December 25th and January 1st and those days are considered part of the employees' vacation time.

  Companies also can set the number of allowable sick days per year. If this is part of the offer, then it's important to understand what happens if you come down with the Swine Flu and can't go to work for a week. If you only get four sick days per year, does the fifth day get taken out of your vacation time? Some companies won't set a number of days, but have policies related to short term disability if a person is out of work for a certain number of consecutive days.

* **401K/pension and Mileage reimbursement or car allowance or company car**
Each organization will have set policies on these based on the structure of the company. This will be covered in greater detail in the "negotiable" and "non-negotiable" section of the book.

* **'Signing bonus'**
Not every offer will have one of these, but in certain industries or professions they can be very common and more available in larger companies. A signing bonus can be intended to compensate someone who will be leaving a position which they could expect to receive a 'bonus' if they stayed through the end of a month, quarter, or year. Sales, management, or operational positions could reasonably expect to have a signing bonus be part of the job offer.

Most signing bonuses come with language in the document you "sign" which could state that if you leave the company within a certain period of time (most often 12 months), you would have to pay the 'signing bonus' back to the company. This shouldn't be a concern as long as you are evaluating the offer completely and making a decision to accept the offer based on the total package. Hopefully you will be making a careful and thoughtful decision to accept a career opportunity and won't be moving to another company within a year.

* **Relocation allowance or reimbursement**
Similar to the 'signing bonus' there can be a document which says repayment is due if you leave the company before a certain period of time. In the 'negotiable' section of the book we will

discuss more details around what would be appropriate to ask regarding relocation packages.

◆ **Timing of performance evaluation and merit increases** Performance evaluations or reviews will be specific to the company's policies. More details on these benefits will be in the 'non-negotiable' and 'negotiable' sections of the book.

Overall, the more information you can get about the details of an offer, the better prepared you will be to evaluate what is 'good' and what could potentially be clarified or negotiated.

• • •

My knowledge of what is 'negotiable' is strong I think ...

Not everything is 'negotiable' in a job offer. Some parts of the offer are going to be 'fixed' based on company policy. Companies have to offer 'fair' compensation packages and benefits to employees, so some things may be written as formal policies for everyone.

Here are some general guidelines on how to determine what may be 'negotiable':

- Information on salary and bonus structure was posted in the job description
  - If a company has openly shared a flat (as opposed to a range) salary or bonus publicly, the potential to negotiate this is going to be less. By putting it in writing the company has set the expectation to you in advance to avoid going through negotiation.

- Someone in the interview process reviewed details of the health benefits package with you already
  - Medical and dental and vision benefits themselves are usually not negotiable since companies establish those through large health insurance companies. The timing of the start of benefits may be negotiable depending on the medical carrier, your personal situation for 'bridge coverage' from your current employer, or the level of the position within the organization.

- You asked a specific question about performance-based evaluations in the interview process
  - In the 'Questions to Ask in an Interview', you asked the hiring person about when you would be evaluated on performance and they stated you would receive an annual review and merit increases are based on that evaluation. In this case, it is probably company policy so the organization can plan set timing and percentages for salary increases (outside of promotions). Asking for the company to go outside of policy to review your performance earlier for additional compensation would not be realistic.
  - It would be reasonable, depending on the position and the manager to request a review earlier to evaluate whether you are 'on track' for a positive performance evaluation. Some large companies have instituted 'mid-year' reviews to set expectations and allow for employees to adjust performance for more positive annual evaluations.

The purpose of asking for the offer in writing is to see the specifics of the compensation package – and hiring managers and human resource directors consider 'compensation' everything you receive from a company. When you are evaluating the written offer, it's important to determine what information is there and what may be 'missing' that you need to ask questions about.

For example, maybe there is a notation on the offer -'Health Benefits'- but no details about timing for the start of coverage. Vacation time and how you earn it may not be listed. Participation in the 401K or pension plan might be vague. Consider all of the items on the previous list and see what gaps there are in the information provided in the written offer.

Negotiation doesn't have to be 'asking for more'. It could be clarifying and requesting a different timeline. You may 'negotiate' a later start date so you can take some time off between positions. Possibly you have a trip scheduled later in the year and you want to have extra days of vacation 'accrue' to be able to use them then. Maybe the signing bonus is less than you could potentially receive if you were 'on track' for more in your current position – do your homework on this one first – then you could possibly request additional compensation here.

Below are some commonly 'negotiated' parts of an offer – be cautious about this though, because not everything is up for discussion and it is important to choose the compensation items that are most important to you to negotiate first.

- **Salary**
  - If you know from the company that there is a 'range' offered, and your skills would justify being given a higher salary in the range than what was offered to you, then salary can be negotiated. In most cases the hiring manager will find out what your current salary is in order to make a competitive offer to you. Salary could also potentially be negotiated if the offer is lower than your current pay and you can justify and prove that to the employer.

- **Timing of health benefits to start**
  - Company policies or contracts with the healthcare company may or may not allow for this.

- **Vacation allowance timing**
  - This may or may not be negotiable depending on the company policy. The best time to negotiate this is if you already have a trip planned and you can establish that right away with the company to have the time off. Negotiating to get vacation early without a plan could seem unnecessary.

- **Mileage vs. car allowance vs. company car**
  - Each company will have policies around this that could change from year to year. Asking if you could get a car allowance instead of a company car could be a reasonable request. Be prepared that the company could have corporate reasons for only giving one or the other.

- **Car allowance**
  - If you are offered a car allowance you may be able to negotiate the amount if you can justify your current compensation in this area is higher than what is being offered. Requesting a higher amount to buy a more luxurious vehicle than what you currently have would only be realistic if the standard car the other employees in the position are driving is nicer than your current vehicle.

- **Guaranteed 'Bonus' compensation**
  - This could be negotiated if the position you are leaving had a set bonus structure that you are leaving and the new opportunity will not guarantee your bonus or has a time gap which would not offer a bonus (i.e.: first 6 months no bonus is available since it is considered a probation period).
  - Usually negotiating this would be for a set period of time; the first quarter or up to one year after being hired.

- **Signing bonus amount**
  - Be aware that this will most likely have a 'repayment' factor for leaving the company before a certain time of employment.

- **Relocation allowance or reimbursement**
  - This also will most likely have a 'repayment' factor for leaving the company early.

- Relocation amounts may be 'fixed' by geography or distance relocating ('non-negotiable' section)
- Since relocation is usually handled by an outside company, the amounts may also be restricted based on the contracts with the provider.

- **Start date**
  - Delaying your start date may be appropriate, but remember that the company projects several dynamics around when they offer a start date, including salary costs, training class timing, allocation of workload in departments, etc.
  - Having a reason such as completion of another project or responsibility at your current position or wanting to 'transition' the person replacing you could be good reasons for a delay. You can ask for a delay but a pre-planned reason will give you a greater chance to get it.

- **Timing of performance review**
  - The size of the organization could depend on how negotiable this point is — small to medium size companies may be able to determine timing on a sliding 'start date' scale.

It's also important to note that you don't need to negotiate anything in some cases. Companies may not give you all the information you need and then it is definitely important to ask questions to understand the offer completely. If the offer has all of the parts you need to make a career decision, then don't feel compelled to have something to negotiate.

• • •

My assessment of what is

'non-negotiable' is reasonable I think ...

'Non-negotiable' items in an offer are also dependent on the size of the organization, company dynamics that year, industry standards, and other factors like geography. Salary may be 'non-negotiable' because the company has set levels for the position in given geographies each year. If the company just contracted with X car manufacturer and Y car insurance company to get company cars for all of the salespeople, the chances of getting a car allowance would be significantly lower.

General 'non-negotiable' parts of positions could include:

- **Level of Health Benefits**
  - Most companies negotiate contracts with insurers on these, so they are set for all employees.
  - This will also include which providers are covered, so if maintaining your current healthcare providers is important, investigate what ways you could do that and use options through the employer to gain reimbursement. Out of network coverage or 'fee for service negotiation' may be a couple of options if the provider is not 'on contract' with the insurer.

- **Sick Day Benefits**
  - If the company has listed allowable number of sick days, then it is a company policy which is non-modifiable. It's good to understand sick day and short term disability policies in advance of acceptance of the offer.

- **Insurance Benefits**
  - These are contracted most of the time through a third party and will be standard for all employees in a company. The level of the position within the company may dictate the level of coverage and percentage contributed automatically by the company versus contributions needed by the employee.
  - Along with insurance, some organizations may provide an Employee Assistance program which could include counseling or therapy or other services. These would also be 'non-negotiable' since the programs are usually contracted at set levels with a third party.

- **'Bonus' compensation**
  - Unless you are entering a commission based position (and even those are usually non-negotiable percentage based), don't try to negotiate this. Companies do fiscal projections on scales and bell curves for bonus payouts so they are fixed in advance.
  - Positions that receive an annual bonus based on overall company performance also will be pre-determined, and percentages of payouts are usually distributed for whatever level the company achieves versus set annual goals.

- **401K and pension/retirement plans**
  - Timing to contribute into these, amount you can contribute, and whether a company even offers these is already pre-determined through contracts with providers and federal guidelines.

- **Mileage reimbursement**
  - The amount of mileage reimbursement is set by the federal government each year. Most companies will follow this guideline.

- ◆ **Company car**
  - Organizations that offer a company car contract with large manufacturers to get discounts. So the chances of getting a Lexus when the company contracts for a Malibu are not very high.

- ◆ **Business expense reimbursement**
  - You will either get this, or not. It really depends on what your job description is and what company policy is on what is considered a 'business expense' or not. Meals when travelling, accommodations, office supplies, etc. could be included. Instead of negotiating this, it's a good idea to ask questions about what is generally classified as 'business expense' and what is reasonable for consideration in the position you are interviewing for.

- ◆ **Geographic location of the position**
  - This may be negotiable as long as they haven't asked you previously where you prefer to be located. Companies plan this out before they extend offers, so the hiring manager may be offering different geographies at the same time to several people.
  - If the position is listed as 'multiple locations nationally', this would be a great question to ask in the last stages of the interview process. By discussing your preference in geography with the hiring manager in advance, you can eliminate any confusion or need to negotiate this in the offer process.

• • •

<inline_image description="small circular logo reading 'I think'" />

My understanding of who to discuss negotiable points with is accurate I think...

The first point to consider is who called and offered you the job? In larger organizations, a human resources person will make the actual offer because those people are experts in answering questions about the different parts of the compensation package. Some companies have the hiring manager (who you will be reporting to) call – they can tell you how excited they are to have you 'join the team'. Smaller companies may have the Owner contact you to give the offer and then have an office manager or other department head follow up with the details.

Ultimately, the person who contacts you is the first one to follow up with once you have read the written offer. Before you call the person, be sure to prepare:

- Notes on a pad of paper with the categories of the offer that you have questions about
  - This includes items that you need more information or clarification on, not necessarily items to negotiate.

- List – in order of importance to you – of parts you want to negotiate
  - Planning out what you are going to ask for will allow you to be methodical and professional in how you request changes to the original offer. It is crucial not to just ask for 'a later start date' – have an exact date you want to change to and be prepared to give a rationale why you are asking for it.

- This doesn't mean you have to give graphic details on the project that needs to be completed in your current role and why you are asking for a delayed start date. General explanation of your role and the commitment that you have made to that manager and department is appropriate.

When you call the person who made you the offer, establish that you are calling to get more information on parts of the offer. At that point, they may tell you to call someone else, which is fine. If they do not, then start the conversation letting them know you have taken time to review the offer and show appreciation for receiving it. Go through the items you have questions about first and take detailed notes. If you are going to try and negotiate, then start with the most important item first.

The company can always tell you no to the things you ask for. The better you have planned a rationale for the request, the greater your chances of getting it, or at least moved closer to what you want. It's very important to ask for negotiated parts of the offer – don't be perceived as 'telling or demanding' something. The difference is using "could I" or "is it possible to" instead of "I need to" or "I can't" when you make the request. Negotiation should not be emotional either. Sharing personal information about why you are requesting a higher salary, such as a financial commitment (mortgage or rent cost) would not be appropriate.

The person may have to get back to you on items you want to have modified. Some items might be 'non-negotiable' and you won't know until you ask. Once you get answers back on your questions and, if applicable, negotiated points, then it is time to make a decision. If you are interviewing with multiple companies then you have to start evaluating a number of variables. By keeping accurate notes throughout the interview process with each company will help to make the decision time much easier and less complicated.

• • •

My timeline for making a decision is appropriate for the company I think...

At this point in the process, you've talked to the right person and asked questions about the details of the offer. After presenting your reasons for wanting to negotiate on a couple of items, you were given reasons you could or could not have what you asked for. Now the company will want to know if you are going to accept or reject the offer.

When the person first made you an offer, they probably told you when the company 'needed to hear back from you'. The time between receiving the written offer and asking questions or negotiating, or both, may have gone past the original timing they wanted an answer in. If that's the case, you may have a shortened period of time to make a decision.

The key to knowing what your timeline for acceptance or rejection of an offer depends on your communication with the person you are having offer discussions with. It is very important to communicate consistently with the hiring manager or HR person during the offer evaluation process. This will avoid the impression that you are leaving the employer guessing on when they will know whether you are going to commit or not. Employers set deadlines for acceptance in order to limit the delay to contact an alternate candidate with an offer.

Getting back to a company within a week is realistic. When evaluating multiple offers at the same time, you can communicate to the company that you request an extension to respond, beyond a week if necessary, and explain that you are evaluating multiple offers and are very interested in their offer.

If the organization sets a deadline though, it is important not to push it or you could be perceived as unprofessional. Waiting until noon on a Friday, when Friday is the final day to accept or reject an offer, just is not necessary unless you were waiting to hear from your 'first choice' company and that was as soon as you heard from them. By giving an answer as soon as you can to a company, you are being respectful of their hiring process and allowing them to move forward one way or another.

. . .

My views on what compensation is realistic for the position are correct **I think** ....

Depending on what level your position is in the organization and what skills and experience you bring to the position, you should change your expectations of what compensation is realistic. Everyone would love to earn a six figure salary, have a significant car allowance, make a large quarterly bonus or commission, get a raise every six months, and have full benefits with a 401K, pension, and company stock. For most positions below executive or upper management level, receiving all of these things in an offer is not realistic.

In general, realistic compensation items for career opportunities will include:

- ◆ Salary that is fair for the market value of the responsibilities of the job, including industry standards and consideration of cost of living in the geography of the area
  - Someone living in CA or NY would probably earn more than someone living in ID with the same job description and title in the same company. Each company will determine what those differences are annually.
  - To find a general range for this information, go to CBSalary®. It's a search program through Career Builder® which takes into consideration geography, responsibilities etc. This is a good step to do before receiving an offer and once you feel confident that you may be receiving one.

- Benefits (healthcare, dental, insurance) or an option to pay for benefits through the company
- Vacation time
- Reimbursement for company expenses (office supplies if 'at home' office, mileage, business travel etc.)
- Performance review after a set period of time

Those are fairly standard categories for most positions. Each industry will have other offer parts that would be considered 'fair and equitable'. Look at similar opportunities with other companies that are posted through professional association networks, job search engines or company internal websites to identify what else may be realistic for your specific field.

• • •

My process for rejecting an offer
is professional I think ....

After you have taken the time to evaluate the offer details, you have decided that the company, the position responsibilities or the key parts of the offer are not what you want. The most important things to remember about rejecting an offer include:

- Respect the company's timeline and let them know as soon as possible.
  - Remember that they may have a 'second choice' candidate that the management would go to in case you did not accept. The earlier you reject the offer, the higher the odds that the company can still fill the position with a qualified candidate that has also been through the interview process completely, rather than having to start all over.

- Always reject an offer via phone – do not leave a voice mail – talk to the person live. Email is also not appropriate.
- Let the company know why you are rejecting the offer.
  - If the reason is that you have another offer that you have decided to accept, you don't have to go into the details, but let them know that. Wouldn't it be great if companies would tell you why they chose someone besides you to interview? Giving a broad reason like "I have decided to accept another offer that will allow me to expand my managerial skills." is appropriate and professional.

- If you are rejecting because they didn't meet your negotiation points, then you can simply say "I have chosen to pursue other opportunities at this point that will offer a different compensation package."

- ◆ Don't burn any bridges!
  - Depending on the field you are going into, you someday may end up working with, or for, the management whose offer you reject. Thank the recruiter or hiring manager for the opportunity to learn more about the organization and for their time during the interview process. This shows your professionalism in the industry for any future consideration of opportunities.

When you have contacted the person to reject the offer, it is appropriate to follow up in writing via a brief email. Again, this should show appreciation for their time. Another tip includes emailing any managers that you interviewed with and letting them know your decision and appreciation for their time. Those managers may have openings in the future that they could consider you for depending on how you manage the rejection of the offer. If you email the managers, wait until a day after you speak with the recruiter or HR person – this lets them do their job and inform management of your decision.

• • •

My acceptance of an offer shows
careful consideration **I think** ....

Once you have determined it's a good offer, and you are ready to commit – call the person you discussed the offer with. Be sure your questions have been answered first so you feel confident about the position and the compensation package. When you make the call, remember to:

- Thank the person for the opportunity to work for the company.
- Ask when and how the company wants you to complete the final steps in the offer process
  - This could potentially include a drug test, physical, authorization for a driver's record check, signing bonus or relocation package agreement form, and/or completion of an I-9 form.

- Confirm your start date and location/time you are to be 'at the office' (worksite etc.).

What if the company wants you to 'sign' an agreement of acceptance? Whether you are receiving a signing bonus or not, it is very common for companies to ask for a written confirmation which acknowledges that you have accepted the offer. This verifies that you have read the offer and understand all of the sections.

An agreement of acceptance is not a 'contract'. Until you have shown up for your first day of work, your first official day 'on the payroll', you are not employed. If you accept a signing bonus or relocation package funds prior to your first day, and you for whatever reason do not go to work at that company, you could be responsible for paying back that money.

As you would for rejecting an offer, follow up with an email to the person you spoke with to confirm your excitement about the opportunity and details about the next steps and start date.

• • •

My notification to other employers that I am no longer available is appropriate I think ....

Notifying other companies that you have started the interview process with that you are not going to be available to continue in the process is a really important step. This goes along with 'not burning bridges' in the rejection section of the book. The reality is that every industry's recruiters and hiring managers could somehow know each other. We potentially are members of similar organizations, interact at national conferences, or network with each other to set standards for hiring practices and compensation.

If you fail to inform a company that you have accepted another offer, there is a high probability that other companies in the field could hear about it. It doesn't take long to notify people when you aren't going forward with their company, so here are some different situations and specific tips to have the most professional approach:

- You have been contacted by the company for a phone interview, but have accepted another offer before the phone interview takes place
  - In this case, you could email the person who scheduled the phone interview with you and simply state: "I have decided to accept an offer from another organization at this time. Thank you for considering my qualifications for the position."

- You have had a phone interview and are 'waiting' to hear back about the company scheduling a live interview with you

- Same scenario as above, but in this case, you should call the person you had the phone interview with if you have their number. If you don't have their phone number, then you could email them.

♦ You have had a live interview and are 'waiting' to see if you are going to the second round of interviews
  - In this situation, it is VERY important to contact the person who held the live interview with you via phone. Don't leave a message on voicemail.
  - If you absolutely cannot reach the person who interviewed you, you could contact the human resources person (if applicable) and talk live to them.

♦ You have been through all of the interviews, but have not received an offer yet
  - Probably this company would be a 'second choice' for you if you had an offer from them. It's important to contact the company asap once you accept another offer so you keep the 'door open' for possible positions in the future. Again, live contact to the person you have had the most contact with through the interview process at this point.
  - Also, you could contact the managers you interviewed with a day later to thank them for their time in the interview process.

♦ You have been through all of the interviews, and have an offer from them and another company
  - This is the most difficult situation because you are probably pretty interested in this company at this point. You may even have had a hard time choosing between companies. Contact should be live with at least the person you have been communicating with the most during the process.
  - Depending on how much of a connection you made with the other people who interviewed you, you could contact

them via phone or email to show appreciation for their time and keep the door open for the future.

- You have been interviewing internally in multiple departments for positions
  - Since you are going to stay in the organization, being open with the management about what department you decided to accept the offer from is crucial. Contact all of the people you interviewed with in person and follow up via email to thank them for their time in the process.

• • •

'My job offer negotiation skills are solid I think ... so why didn't I get anything I asked for?' ©

Here's a final checklist to help make sure you are managing the offer evaluation, rejection, and acceptance processes with the highest level of professionalism:

- Before returning a call to an employer who may be making an offer, you are in a quiet place and have a pad and pen to take notes
- During the 'offer call', ask for written details of the offer to evaluate all of the parts
- After receiving the written offer, evaluate each of the parts and see what questions need to be answered about details or more information in different sections
- Determine what is 'negotiable' vs. 'non-negotiable'
- Contact the person who made the offer within a reasonable amount of time and determine their timeline for needing an answer or ask for a time period based on considering alternate offers
- Follow up to reject or accept the offer ASAP
- Inform other companies or departments once you have accepted an offer that you are no longer available to hire

After you accept an offer, be sure to celebrate! Congratulations on successfully working through the interview process. Interviewing is a lifelong skill and negotiation will be a skill that you will use throughout your career – for promotions, moves into different departments in a company, changes in industries, or even geographic moves within an organization.

• • •

'My job offer negotiation skills are solid I think ... so why didn't I get anything I asked for?' ©

Extra Resources:

Publications and Professional Associations

- Depending on the industry, there may be specific ways to improve your negotiation skills through publications or professional associations or organizations.

www.bestresumebuilder.com

- If you want to use a program which will walk you through creation of a dynamic resume, step by step, in less than 45 minutes, check out this resource. This may help you focus your interview answers to the 'bullet points' on your resume.

• • •

INDEX

• • •

Other Books in the I think™ Career Skills Series:

Coming Soon in the I think™ Career Skills Series:

'My social networking skills are amazing I think....so why can't I find a job?' ©

AND

'My interview preparation was detailed I think...so why didn't I feel prepared once I got there?' ©

Available Online and In Stores Fall 2010!

• • •

ACKNOWLEDGEMENTS

Thank you to the human resources and management personnel over the past two decades who have offered insight on what can and can't be negotiated based on the job, company, market trends, industry competitiveness, and corporate reality.

• • •

ABOUT THE AUTHOR

Stacie Garlieb is the author of 'My resume is great
I think ... so why didn't I get the interview?'© and 'My
interview skills are strong I think ... so why didn't
I get a job offer?'© As the President of Successful
Impressions, LLC, she assists working professionals
with career search processes and skills. She has been
featured several times on NBC television and KFYI
radio during morning and evening news with interview
tips. In partnership with University of Phoenix, Stacie is
the creator and presenter for the 'Career Workshop

Series' on resume building, interview preparation, interview skills,
social media networking, and 're-careering' and transition in the
workforce.

Stacie has been a seminar speaker for 'Build Your Career Event' (Career
Builder/University of Phoenix) and the Arizona Women's Expo. Her
career search tips and interview skills advice have been published in
national sorority and university alumni publications. Through group
presentations and one-on-one coaching on all career search related
topics, she has worked with public and private college students
nationally since 1991. In collaboration with businesses in various fields,
she actively develops internship programs and recruits at public and
private universities as well as career fairs.

Stacie was invited by California State Sacramento and University of the
Pacific to act as a Career Consultant to the career services departments.
She developed the Career Fair Training Program for University of the Pacific,
and assisted in writing the "Career Services Interview Skills" guide. Over
more than twenty years, she has worked for Fortune 500 organizations in
sales, marketing, and management positions with recruiting responsibility
after earning her Bachelor of Science from Arizona State University.

*If you would like to know more about Stacie Garlieb's company or her
seminars please visit her website at www.successfulimpressions.net*

I think

www.ingramcontent.com/pod-product-compliance
Lightning Source LLC
Chambersburg PA
CBHW051254170526
45165CB00004B/1716